Tao Te Ching

—

Tao Te Ching
by
Lao Tzŭ
J. Legge, Translator

Tao Te Ching
by
Lao Tzŭ
J. Legge, Translator

Edited by C.S. Moore.
Copyright © 2010 by C.S. Moore
All Rights Reserved.
All Rights Reserved. No part of this book may be reproduced
in any form including electronic or mechanical,
photocopying, recording or stored in any format without
written permission from the publisher:

Orkos Press
New York

ISBN: 1-59232-573-4

PRINTED IN THE UNITED STATES OF AMERICA

1

The Tao that can be trodden is not the enduring
and
unchanging Tao. The name that can be named is
not the enduring and
unchanging name.

(Conceived of as) having no name, it is the
Originator of heaven
and earth; (conceived of as) having a name, it is
the Mother of all
things.

Always without desire we must be found,
If its deep mystery we would sound;
But if desire always within us be,
Its outer fringe is all that we shall see.

Under these two aspects, it is really the same; but
as development
takes place, it receives the different names.
Together we call them
the Mystery. Where the Mystery is the deepest is
the gate of all that
is subtle and wonderful.

2

All in the world know the beauty of the beautiful,
and in doing
this they have (the idea of) what ugliness is; they
all know the skill
of the skillful, and in doing this they have (the
idea of) what the
want of skill is.

So it is that existence and non-existence give birth
the one to
(the idea of) the other; that difficulty and ease
produce the one (the
idea of) the other; that length and shortness
fashion out the one the
figure of the other; that (the ideas of) height and
lowness arise from
the contrast of the one with the other; that the
musical notes and
tones become harmonious through the relation of
one with another; and
that being before and behind give the idea of one
following another.

Therefore the sage manages affairs without doing
anything, and
conveys his instructions without the use of
speech.

All things spring up, and there is not one which
declines to show

itself; they grow, and there is no claim made for
their ownership;
they go through their processes, and there is no
expectation (of a
reward for the results). The work is accomplished,
and there is no
resting in it (as an achievement).

The work is done, but how no one can see;
'Tis this that makes the power not cease to be.

3

Not to value and employ men of superior ability is
the way to
keep the people from rivalry among themselves;
not to prize articles
which are difficult to procure is the way to keep
them from becoming
thieves; not to show them what is likely to excite
their desires is
the way to keep their minds from disorder.

Therefore the sage, in the exercise of his
government, empties
their minds, fills their bellies, weakens their wills,
and strengthens
their bones.

He constantly (tries to) keep them without
knowledge and without
desire, and where there are those who have
knowledge, to keep them
from presuming to act (on it). When there is this
abstinence from
action, good order is universal.

4

The Tao is (like) the emptiness of a vessel; and in
our
employment of it we must be on our guard against
all fulness. How
deep and unfathomable it is, as if it were the
Honored Ancestor of
all things!

We should blunt our sharp points, and unravel the
complications of
things; we should temper our brightness, and
bring ourselves into
agreement with the obscurity of others. How pure
and still the Tao
is, as if it would ever so continue!

I do not know whose son it is. It might appear to
have been before
God.

5

Heaven and earth do not act from (the impulse of)
any wish to be
benevolent; they deal with all things as the dogs
of grass are dealt
with. The sages do not act from (any wish to be)
benevolent; they
deal with the people as the dogs of grass are dealt
with.

May not the space between heaven and earth be
compared to a
bellows?

'Tis emptied, yet it loses not its power;
'Tis moved again, and sends forth air the more.
Much speech to swift exhaustion lead we see;
Your inner being guard, and keep it free.

6

The valley spirit dies not, aye the same;
The female mystery thus do we name.
Its gate, from which at first they issued forth,
Is called the root from which grew heaven and
earth.
Long and unbroken does its power remain,
Used gently, and without the touch of pain.

7

Heaven is long-enduring and earth continues long.
The reason
why heaven and earth are able to endure and
continue thus long is
because they do not live of, or for, themselves.
This is how they are
able to continue and endure.

Therefore the sage puts his own person last, and
yet it is found in
the foremost place; he treats his person as if it
were foreign to him,
and yet that person is preserved. Is it not because
he has no
personal and private ends, that therefore such ends
are realized?

8

The highest excellence is like (that of) water. The excellence
of water appears in its benefiting all things, and in
its occupying,
without striving (to the contrary), the low place
which all men
dislike. Hence (its way) is near to (that of) the
Tao.

The excellence of a residence is in (the suitability
of) the place;
that of the mind is in abysmal stillness; that of
associations is in
their being with the virtuous; that of government
is in its securing
good order; that of (the conduct of) affairs is in its
ability; and
that of (the initiation of) any movement is in its
timeliness.

And when (one with the highest excellence) does
not wrangle (about
his low position), no one finds fault with him.

9

It is better to leave a vessel unfilled, than to attempt to
carry it when it is full. If you keep feeling a point that has been
sharpened, the point cannot long preserve its sharpness.

When gold and jade fill the hall, their possessor cannot keep them
safe. When wealth and honors lead to arrogance, this brings its evil
on itself. When the work is done, and one's name is becoming
distinguished, to withdraw into obscurity is the way of Heaven.

10

When the intelligent and animal souls are held
together in one
embrace, they can be kept from separating. When
one gives undivided
attention to the (vital) breathe, and brings it to the
utmost degree of
pliancy, he can become as a (tender) babe. When
he has cleansed away
the most mysterious sights (of his imagination),
he can become without
a flaw.

In loving the people and ruling the state, cannot
he proceed
without any (purpose of) action? In the opening
and shutting of his
gates of heaven, cannot he do so as a female bird?
While his
intelligence reaches in every direction, cannot he
(appear to) be
without knowledge?

(The Tao) produces (all things) and nourishes
them; it produces
them and does not claim them as its own; it does
all, and yet does not
boast of it; it presides over all, and yet does not
control them.
This is what is called 'The mysterious Quality' (of
the Tao).

11

The thirty spokes unite in the one nave; but it is
on the empty
space (for the axle), that the use of the wheel
depends. Clay is
fashioned into vessels; but it is on their empty
hollowness, that
their use depends. The door and windows are cut
out (from the walls)
to form an apartment; but it is on the empty space
(within), that its
use depends. Therefore, what has a (positive)
existence serves for
profitable adaptation, and what has not that for
(actual) usefulness.

12

Color's five hues from th' eyes their sight will
take;
Music's five notes the ears as deaf can make;
The flavors five deprive the mouth of taste;
The chariot course, and the wild hunting waste
Make mad the mind; and objects rare and strange,
Sought for, men's conduct will to evil change.

Therefore the sage seeks to satisfy (the craving of)
the belly, and
not the (insatiable longing of the) eyes. He puts
from him the
latter, and prefers to seek the former.

13

Favor and disgrace would seem equally to be
feared; honor and
great calamity, to be regarded as personal
conditions (of the same
kind).

What is meant by speaking thus of favor and
disgrace? Disgrace is
being in a low position (after the enjoyment of
favor). The getting
that (favor) leads to the apprehension (of losing
it), and the losing
it leads to the fear of (still greater calamity):--this
is what is
meant by saying that favor and disgrace would
seem equally to be
feared.

And what is meant by saying that honor and great
calamity are to be
(similarly) regarded as personal conditions? What
makes me liable to
great calamity is my having the body (which I call
myself); if I had
not the body, what great calamity could come to
me?

Therefore he who would administer the kingdom,
honoring it as he
honors his own person, may be employed to

govern it, and he who would
administer it with the love which he bears to his
own person may be
entrusted with it.

14

We look at it, and we do not see it, and we name it
'the
Equable.' We listen to it, and we do not hear it,
and we name it 'the
Inaudible.' We try to grasp it, and do not get hold
of it, and we
name it 'the Subtle.' With these three qualities, it
cannot be made
the subject of description; and hence we blend
them together and
obtain The One.

Its upper part is not bright, and its lower part is
not obscure.
Ceaseless in its action, it yet cannot be named,
and then it again
returns and becomes nothing. This is called the
Form of the Formless,
and the Semblance of the Invisible; this is called
the Fleeting and
Indeterminable.

We meet it and do not see its Front; we follow it,
and do not see
its Back. When we can lay hold of the Tao of old
to direct the things
of the present day, and are able to know it as it
was of old in the
beginning, this is called (unwinding) the clue of
Tao.

15

The skillful masters (of the Tao) in old times, with
a subtle
and exquisite penetration, comprehended its
mysteries, and were deep
(also) so as to elude men's knowledge. As they
were thus beyond men's
knowledge, I will make an effort to describe of
what sort they
appeared to be.

Shrinking looked they like those who wade
through a stream in
winter; irresolute like those who are afraid of all
around them; grave
like a guest (in awe of his host); evanescent like
ice that is melting
away; unpretentious like wood that has not been
fashioned into
anything; vacant like a valley, and dull like
muddy water.

Who can (make) the muddy water (clear)? Let it
be still, and it
will gradually become clear. Who can secure the
condition of rest?
Let movement go on, and the condition of rest
will gradually arise.

They who preserve this method of the Tao do not
wish to be full (of

themselves). It is through their not being full of themselves that
they can afford to seem worn and not appear new and complete.

16

The (state of) vacancy should be brought to the
utmost degree,
and that of stillness guarded with unwearying
vigor. All things
alike go through their processes of activity, and
(then) we see them
return (to their original state). When things (in the
vegetable
world) have displayed their luxuriant growth, we
see each of them
return to its root. This returning to their root is
what we call the
state of stillness; and that stillness may be called a
reporting that
they have fulfilled their appointed end.

The report of that fulfilment is the regular,
unchanging rule. To
know that unchanging rule is to be intelligent; not
to know it leads
to wild movements and evil issues. The
knowledge of that unchanging
rule produces a (grand) capacity and forbearance,
and that capacity
and forbearance lead to a community (of feeling
with all things).
From this community of feeling comes a
kingliness of character; and he
who is king-like goes on to be heaven-like. In that
likeness to

heaven he possesses the Tao. Possessed of the
Tao, he endures long;
and to the end of his bodily life, is exempt from
all danger of decay.

17

In the highest antiquity, (the people) did not know
that there
were (their rulers). In the next age they loved
them and praised
them. In the next they feared them; in the next
they despised them.
Thus it was that when faith (in the Tao) was
deficient (in the rulers)
a want of faith in them ensued (in the people).

How irresolute did those (earliest rulers) appear,
showing (by
their reticence) the importance which they set
upon their words!
Their work was done and their undertakings were
successful, while the
people all said, 'We are as we are, of ourselves!'

18

When the Great Tao (Way or Method) ceased to
be observed,
benevolence and righteousness came into vogue.
(Then) appeared wisdom
and shrewdness, and there ensued great hypocrisy.

When harmony no longer prevailed throughout
the six kinships,
filial sons found their manifestation; when the
states and clans fell
into disorder, loyal ministers appeared.

19

If we could renounce our sageness and discard our
wisdom, it
would be better for the people a hundredfold. If
we could renounce
our benevolence and discard our righteousness,
the people would again
become filial and kindly. If we could renounce
our artful
contrivances and discard our (scheming for) gain,
there would be no
thieves nor robbers.

Those three methods (of government)
Thought olden ways in elegance did fail
And made these names their want of worth to veil;
But simple views, and courses plain and true
Would selfish ends and many lusts eschew.

20

When we renounce learning we have no troubles.
The (ready) 'yes,' and (flattering) 'yea;'--
Small is the difference they display.
But mark their issues, good and ill;--
What space the gulf between shall fill?

What all men fear is indeed to be feared; but how
wide and without end
is the range of questions (asking to be discussed)!

The multitude of men look satisfied and pleased;
as if enjoying a
full banquet, as if mounted on a tower in spring. I
alone seem
listless and still, my desires having as yet given no
indication of
their presence. I am like an infant which has not
yet smiled. I look
dejected and forlorn, as if I had no home to go to.
The multitude of
men all have enough and to spare. I alone seem to
have lost
everything. My mind is that of a stupid man; I am
in a state of
chaos.

Ordinary men look bright and intelligent, while I
alone seem to be
benighted. They look full of discrimination, while
I alone am dull

and confused. I seem to be carried about as on the sea, drifting as if I had nowhere to rest. All men have their spheres of action, while I alone seem dull and incapable, like a rude borderer. (Thus) I alone am different from other men, but I value the nursing-mother (the Tao).

21

The grandest forms of active force
From Tao come, their only source.
Who can of Tao the nature tell?
Our sight it flies, our touch as well.
Eluding sight, eluding touch,
The forms of things all in it crouch;
Eluding touch, eluding sight,
There are their semblances, all right.
Profound it is, dark and obscure;
Things' essences all there endure.
Those essences the truth enfold
Of what, when seen, shall then be told.
Now it is so; 'twas so of old.
Its name--what passes not away;
So, in their beautiful array,
Things form and never know decay.

How know I that it is so with all the beauties of
existing things? By
this (nature of the Tao).

22

The partial becomes complete; the crooked,
straight; the empty,
full; the worn out, new. He whose (desires) are
few gets them; he
whose (desires) are many goes astray.

Therefore the sage holds in his embrace the one
thing (of
humility), and manifests it to all the world. He is
free from self-
display, and therefore he shines; from self-
assertion, and therefore
he is distinguished; from self-boasting, and
therefore his merit is
acknowledged; from self-complacency, and
therefore he acquires
superiority. It is because he is thus free from
striving that
therefore no one in the world is able to strive with
him.

That saying of the ancients that 'the partial
becomes complete' was
not vainly spoken:--all real completion is
comprehended under it.

23

Abstaining from speech marks him who is
obeying the spontaneity
of his nature. A violent wind does not last for a
whole morning; a
sudden rain does not last for the whole day. To
whom is it that these
(two) things are owing? To Heaven and Earth. If
Heaven and Earth
cannot make such (spasmodic) actings last long,
how much less can man!

Therefore when one is making the Tao his
business, those who are
also pursuing it, agree with him in it, and those
who are making the
manifestation of its course their object agree with
him in that; while
even those who are failing in both these things
agree with him where
they fail.

Hence, those with whom he agrees as to the Tao
have the happiness
of attaining to it; those with whom he agrees as to
its manifestation
have the happiness of attaining to it; and those
with whom he agrees
in their failure have also the happiness of attaining
(to the Tao).
(But) when there is not faith sufficient (on his

part), a want of
faith (in him) ensues (on the part of the others).

24

He who stands on his tiptoes does not stand firm;
he who stretches
his legs does not walk (easily). (So), he who
displays himself does
not shine; he who asserts his own views is not
distinguished; he who
vaunts himself does not find his merit
acknowledged; he who is self-
conceited has no superiority allowed to him. Such
conditions, viewed
from the standpoint of the Tao, are like remnants
of food, or a tumor
on the body, which all dislike. Hence those who
pursue (the course)
of the Tao do not adopt and allow them.

25

There was something undefined and complete,
coming into
existence before Heaven and Earth. How still it
was and formless,
standing alone, and undergoing no change,
reaching everywhere and in
no danger (of being exhausted)! It may be
regarded as the Mother of
all things.

I do not know its name, and I give it the
designation of the Tao
(the Way or Course). Making an effort (further) to
give it a name I
call it The Great.

Great, it passes on (in constant flow). Passing on,
it becomes
remote. Having become remote, it returns.
Therefore the Tao is
great; Heaven is great; Earth is great; and the
(sage) king is also
great. In the universe there are four that are great,
and the (sage)
king is one of them.

Man takes his law from the Earth; the Earth takes
its law from
Heaven; Heaven takes its law from the Tao. The

law of the Tao is its
being what it is.

26

Gravity is the root of lightness; stillness, the ruler
of
movement.

Therefore a wise prince, marching the whole day,
does not go far
from his baggage waggons. Although he may
have brilliant prospects to
look at, he quietly remains (in his proper place),
indifferent to
them. How should the lord of a myriad chariots
carry himself lightly
before the kingdom? If he do act lightly, he has
lost his root (of
gravity); if he proceed to active movement, he
will lose his throne.

27

The skillful traveler leaves no traces of his wheels
or
footsteps; the skillful speaker says nothing that
can be found fault
with or blamed; the skillful reckoner uses no
tallies; the skillful
closer needs no bolts or bars, while to open what
he has shut will be
impossible; the skillful binder uses no strings or
knots, while to
unloose what he has bound will be impossible. In
the same way the
sage is always skillful at saving men, and so he
does not cast away any
man; he is always skillful at saving things, and so
he does not cast
away anything. This is called 'Hiding the light of
his procedure.'

Therefore the man of skill is a master (to be
looked up to) by him
who has not the skill; and he who has not the skill
is the helper of
(the reputation of) him who has the skill. If the
one did not honor
his master, and the other did not rejoice in his
helper, an
(observer), though intelligent, might greatly err
about them. This is
called 'The utmost degree of mystery.'

28

Who knows his manhood's strength,
Yet still his female feebleness maintains;
As to one channel flow the many drains,
All come to him, yea, all beneath the sky.
Thus he the constant excellence retains;
The simple child again, free from all stains.

Who knows how white attracts,
Yet always keeps himself within black's shade,
The pattern of humility displayed,
Displayed in view of all beneath the sky;
He in the unchanging excellence arrayed,
Endless return to man's first state has made.

Who knows how glory shines,
Yet loves disgrace, nor e'er for it is pale;
Behold his presence in a spacious vale,
To which men come from all beneath the sky.
The unchanging excellence completes its tale;
The simple infant man in him we hail.

The unwrought material, when divided and
distributed, forms
vessels. The sage, when employed, becomes the
Head of all the
Officers (of government); and in his greatest
regulations he employs
no violent measures.

29

If anyone should wish to get the kingdom for
himself, and to
effect this by what he does, I see that he will not
succeed. The
kingdom is a spirit-like thing, and cannot be got
by active doing. He
who would so win it destroys it; he who would
hold it in his grasp
loses it.

The course and nature of things is such that
What was in front is now behind;
What warmed anon we freezing find.
Strength is of weakness oft the spoil;
The store in ruins mocks our toil.

Hence the sage puts away excessive effort,
extravagance, and easy
indulgence.

30

He who would assist a lord of men in harmony
with the Tao will
not assert his mastery in the kingdom by force of
arms. Such a course
is sure to meet with its proper return.

Wherever a host is stationed, briars and thorns
spring up. In the
sequence of great armies there are sure to be bad
years.

A skillful (commander) strikes a decisive blow,
and stops. He does
not dare (by continuing his operations) to assert
and complete his
mastery. He will strike the blow, but will be on
his guard against
being vain or boastful or arrogant in consequence
of it. He strikes
it as a matter of necessity; he strikes it, but not
from a wish for
mastery.

When things have attained their strong maturity
they become old.
This may be said to be not in accordance with the
Tao: and what is not
in accordance with it soon comes to an end.

31

Now arms, however beautiful, are instruments of
evil omen,
hateful, it may be said, to all creatures. Therefore
they who have
the Tao do not like to employ them.

The superior man ordinarily considers the left
hand the most
honorable place, but in time of war the right hand.
Those sharp
weapons are instruments of evil omen, and not the
instruments of the
superior man;--he uses them only on the
compulsion of necessity. Calm
and repose are what he prizes; victory (by force of
arms) is to him
undesirable. To consider this desirable would be
to delight in the
slaughter of men; and he who delights in the
slaughter of men cannot
get his will in the kingdom.

On occasions of festivity to be on the left hand is
the prized
position; on occasions of mourning, the right
hand. The second in
command of the army has his place on the left; the
general commanding
in chief has his on the right;--his place, that is, is
assigned to him

as in the rites of mourning. He who has killed
multitudes of men
should weep for them with the bitterest grief; and
the victor in
battle has his place (rightly) according to those
rites.

32

The Tao, considered as unchanging, has no name.

Though in its primordial simplicity it may be
small, the whole
world dares not deal with (one embodying) it as a
minister. If a
feudal prince or the king could guard and hold it,
all would
spontaneously submit themselves to him.

Heaven and Earth (under its guidance) unite
together and send down
the sweet dew, which, without the directions of
men, reaches equally
everywhere as of its own accord.

As soon as it proceeds to action, it has a name.
When it once has
that name, (men) can know to rest in it. When
they know to rest in
it, they can be free from all risk of failure and
error.

The relation of the Tao to all the world is like that
of the great
rivers and seas to the streams from the valleys.

33

He who knows other men is discerning; he who
knows himself is
intelligent. He who overcomes others is strong; he
who overcomes
himself is mighty. He who is satisfied with his lot
is rich; he who
goes on acting with energy has a (firm) will.

He who does not fail in the requirements of his
position, continues
long; he who dies and yet does not perish, has
longevity.

34

All-pervading is the Great Tao! It may be found
on the left
hand and on the right.

All things depend on it for their production, which
it gives to
them, not one refusing obedience to it. When its
work is
accomplished, it does not claim the name of
having done it. It
clothes all things as with a garment, and makes no
assumption of being
their lord;--it may be named in the smallest things.
All things
return (to their root and disappear), and do not
know that it is it
which presides over their doing so;--it may be
named in the greatest
things.

Hence the sage is able (in the same way) to
accomplish his great
achievements. It is through his not making
himself great that he can
accomplish them.

35

To him who holds in his hands the Great Image
(of the invisible
Tao), the whole world repairs. Men resort to him,
and receive no
hurt, but (find) rest, peace, and the feeling of ease.

Music and dainties will make the passing guest
stop (for a time).
But though the Tao as it comes from the mouth,
seems insipid and has
no flavour, though it seems not worth being
looked at or listened to,
the use of it is inexhaustible.

36

When one is about to take an inspiration, he is
sure to make a
(previous) expiration; when he is going to weaken
another, he will
first strengthen him; when he is going to
overthrow another, he will
first have raised him up; when he is going to
despoil another, he will
first have made gifts to him:--this is called 'Hiding
the light (of
his procedure).'

The soft overcomes the hard; and the weak the
strong.

Fishes should not be taken from the deep;
instruments for the
profit of a state should not be shown to the people.

37

The Tao in its regular course does nothing (for the sake of
doing it), and so there is nothing which it does not do.

If princes and kings were able to maintain it, all things would of
themselves be transformed by them.

If this transformation became to me an object of desire, I would
express the desire by the nameless simplicity.

Simplicity without a name
Is free from all external aim.
With no desire, at rest and still,
All things go right as of their will.

38

(Those who) possessed in highest degree the
attributes (of the
Tao) did not (seek) to show them, and therefore
they possessed them
(in fullest measure). (Those who) possessed in a
lower degree those
attributes (sought how) not to lose them, and
therefore they did not
possess them (in fullest measure).

(Those who) possessed in the highest degree those
attributes did
nothing (with a purpose), and had no need to do
anything. (Those who)
possessed them in a lower degree were (always)
doing, and had need to
be so doing.

(Those who) possessed the highest benevolence
were (always seeking)
to carry it out, and had no need to be doing so.
(Those who)
possessed the highest righteousness were (always
seeking) to carry it
out, and had need to be so doing.

(Those who) possessed the highest (sense of)
propriety were (always
seeking) to show it, and when men did not
respond to it, they bared

the arm and marched up to them.

Thus it was that when the Tao was lost, its
attributes appeared;
when its attributes were lost, benevolence
appeared; when benevolence
was lost, righteousness appeared; and when
righteousness was lost, the
proprieties appeared.

Now propriety is the attenuated form of leal-
heartedness and good
faith, and is also the commencement of disorder;
swift apprehension is
(only) a flower of the Tao, and is the beginning of
stupidity.

Thus it is that the Great man abides by what is
solid, and eschews
what is flimsy; dwells with the fruit and not with
the flower. It is
thus that he puts away the one and makes choice
of the other.

39

The things which from of old have got the One
(the Tao) are--

Heaven which by it is bright and pure;
Earth rendered thereby firm and sure;
Spirits with powers by it supplied;
Valleys kept full throughout their void
All creatures which through it do live
Princes and kings who from it get
The model which to all they give.

All these are the results of the One (Tao).

If heaven were not thus pure, it soon would rend;
If earth were not thus sure, 'twould break and
bend;
Without these powers, the spirits soon would fail;
If not so filled, the drought would parch each
vale;
Without that life, creatures would pass away;
Princes and kings, without that moral sway,
However grand and high, would all decay.

Thus it is that dignity finds its (firm) root in its
(previous)
meanness, and what is lofty finds its stability in
the lowness (from
which it rises). Hence princes and kings call
themselves 'Orphans,'
'Men of small virtue,' and as 'Carriages without a

nave.' Is not this
an acknowledgment that in their considering
themselves mean they see
the foundation of their dignity? So it is that in the
enumeration of
the different parts of a carriage we do not come on
what makes it
answer the ends of a carriage. They do not wish to
show themselves
elegant-looking as jade, but (prefer) to be coarse-
looking as an
(ordinary) stone.

40

The movement of the Tao
By contraries proceeds;
And weakness marks the course
Of Tao's mighty deeds.

All things under heaven sprang from It as existing
(and named);
that existence sprang from It as non-existent (and
not named).

41

Scholars of the highest class, when they hear
about the Tao,
earnestly carry it into practice. Scholars of the
middle class, when
they have heard about it, seem now to keep it and
now to lose it.
Scholars of the lowest class, when they have
heard about it, laugh
greatly at it. If it were not (thus) laughed at, it
would not be fit
to be the Tao.

Therefore the sentence-makers have thus
expressed themselves:--

'The Tao, when brightest seen, seems light to lack;
Who progress in it makes, seems drawing back;
Its even way is like a rugged track.
Its highest virtue from the vale doth rise;
Its greatest beauty seems to offend the eyes;
And he has most whose lot the least supplies.
Its firmest virtue seems but poor and low;
Its solid truth seems change to undergo;
Its largest square doth yet no corner show
A vessel great, it is the slowest made;
Loud is its sound, but never word it said;
A semblance great, the shadow of a shade.'

The Tao is hidden, and has no name; but it is the
Tao which is

skillful at imparting (to all things what they need)
and making them
complete.

42

The Tao produced One; One produced Two; Two
produced Three;
Three produced All things. All things leave
behind them the Obscurity
(out of which they have come), and go forward to
embrace the
Brightness (into which they have emerged), while
they are harmonized
by the Breath of Vacancy.

What men dislike is to be orphans, to have little
virtue, to be as
carriages without naves; and yet these are the
designations which
kings and princes use for themselves. So it is that
some things are
increased by being diminished, and others are
diminished by being
increased.

What other men (thus) teach, I also teach. The
violent and strong
do not die their natural death. I will make this the
basis of my
teaching.

43

The softest thing in the world dashes against and
overcomes the
hardest; that which has no (substantial) existence
enters where there
is no crevice. I know hereby what advantage
belongs to doing nothing
(with a purpose).

There are few in the world who attain to the
teaching without
words, and the advantage arising from non-action.

44

Or fame or life,
Which do you hold more dear?
Or life or wealth,
To which would you adhere?
Keep life and lose those other things;
Keep them and lose your life:--which brings
Sorrow and pain more near?

Thus we may see,
Who cleaves to fame
Rejects what is more great;
Who loves large stores
Gives up the richer state.

Who is content
Needs fear no shame.
Who knows to stop
Incurs no blame.
From danger free
Long live shall he.

45

Who thinks his great achievements poor
Shall find his vigor long endure.
Of greatest fullness, deemed a void,
Exhaustion ne'er shall stem the tide.
Do thou what's straight still crooked deem;
Thy greatest art still stupid seem,
And eloquence a stammering scream.

Constant action overcomes cold; being still
overcomes heat. Purity
and stillness give the correct law to all under
heaven.

46

When the Tao prevails in the world, they send
back their swift
horses to (draw) the dung-carts. When the Tao is
disregarded in the
world, the war-horses breed in the border lands.

There is no guilt greater than to sanction
ambition; no calamity
greater than to be discontented with one's lot; no
fault greater than
the wish to be getting. Therefore the sufficiency
of contentment is
an enduring and unchanging sufficiency.

47

Without going outside his door, one understands
(all that takes
place) under the sky; without looking out from his
window, one sees
the Tao of Heaven. The farther that one goes out
(from himself), the
less he knows.

Therefore the sages got their knowledge without
travelling; gave
their (right) names to things without seeing them;
and accomplished
their ends without any purpose of doing so.

48

He who devotes himself to learning (seeks) from
day to day to
increase (his knowledge); he who devotes himself
to the Tao (seeks)
from day to day to diminish (his doing).

He diminishes it and again diminishes it, till he
arrives at doing
nothing (on purpose). Having arrived at this point
of non-action,
there is nothing which he does not do.

He who gets as his own all under heaven does so
by giving himself
no trouble (with that end). If one take trouble
(with that end), he
is not equal to getting as his own all under heaven.

49

The sage has no invariable mind of his own; he
makes the mind
of the people his mind.

To those who are good (to me), I am good; and to
those who are not
good (to me), I am also good;--and thus (all) get
to be good. To
those who are sincere (with me), I am sincere; and
to those who are
not sincere (with me), I am also sincere;--and thus
(all) get to be
sincere.

The sage has in the world an appearance of
indecision, and keeps
his mind in a state of indifference to all. The
people all keep their
eyes and ears directed to him, and he deals with
them all as his
children.

50

Men come forth and live; they enter (again) and
die.

Of every ten three are ministers of life (to
themselves); and three
are ministers of death.

There are also three in every ten whose aim is to
live, but whose
movements tend to the land (or place) of death.
And for what reason?
Because of their excessive endeavors to
perpetuate life.

But I have heard that he who is skillful in
managing the life
entrusted to him for a time travels on the land
without having to shun
rhinoceros or tiger, and enters a host without
having to avoid buff
coat or sharp weapon. The rhinoceros finds no
place in him into which
to thrust its horn, nor the tiger a place in which to
fix its claws,
nor the weapon a place to admit its point. And for
what reason?
Because there is in him no place of death.

51

All things are produced by the Tao, and nourished by its
outflowing operation. They receive their forms according to the
nature of each, and are completed according to the circumstances of
their condition. Therefore all things without exception honor the
Tao, and exalt its outflowing operation.

This honoring of the Tao and exalting of its operation is not the
result of any ordination, but always a spontaneous tribute.

Thus it is that the Tao produces (all things), nourishes them,
brings them to their full growth, nurses them, completes them, matures
them, maintains them, and overspreads them.

It produces them and makes no claim to the possession of them; it
carries them through their processes and does not vaunt its ability in
doing so; it brings them to maturity and exercises no control over
them;--this is called its mysterious operation.

52

(The Tao) which originated all under the sky is to
be
considered as the mother of them all.

When the mother is found, we know what her
children should be.
When one knows that he is his mother's child, and
proceeds to guard
(the qualities of) the mother that belong to him, to
the end of his
life he will be free from all peril.

Let him keep his mouth closed, and shut up the
portals (of his
nostrils), and all his life he will be exempt from
laborious exertion.
Let him keep his mouth open, and (spend his
breath) in the promotion
of his affairs, and all his life there will be no
safety for him.

The perception of what is small is (the secret of
clear-
sightedness; the guarding of what is soft and
tender is (the secret
of) strength.

Who uses well his light,
Reverting to its (source so) bright,

Will from his body ward all blight,
And hides the unchanging from men's sight.

53

If I were suddenly to become known, and (put into a position
to) conduct (a government) according to the Great Tao, what I should
be most afraid of would be a boastful display.

The great Tao (or way) is very level and easy; but people love the
by-ways.

Their court (-yards and buildings) shall be well kept, but their
fields shall be ill-cultivated, and their granaries very empty. They
shall wear elegant and ornamented robes, carry a sharp sword at their
girdle, pamper themselves in eating and drinking, and have a
superabundance of property and wealth;--such (princes) may be called
robbers and boasters. This is contrary to the Tao surely!

54

What (Tao's) skillful planter plants
Can never be uptorn;
What his skillful arms enfold,
From him can ne'er be borne.
Sons shall bring in lengthening line,
Sacrifices to his shrine.

Tao when nursed within one's self,
His vigor will make true;
And where the family it rules
What riches will accrue!
The neighborhood where it prevails
In thriving will abound;
And when 'tis seen throughout the state,
Good fortune will be found.
Employ it the kingdom o'er,
And men thrive all around.

In this way the effect will be seen in the person,
by the
observation of different cases; in the family; in the
neighborhood;
in the state; and in the kingdom.

How do I know that this effect is sure to hold thus
all under the
sky? By this (method of observation).

55

He who has in himself abundantly the attributes
(of the Tao) is
like an infant. Poisonous insects will not sting
him; fierce beasts
will not seize him; birds of prey will not strike
him.

(The infant's) bones are weak and its sinews soft,
but yet its
grasp is firm. It knows not yet the union of male
and female, and yet
its virile member may be excited;--showing the
perfection of its
physical essence. All day long it will cry without
its throat
becoming hoarse;--showing the harmony (in its
constitution).

To him by whom this harmony is known,
(The secret of) the unchanging (Tao) is shown,
And in the knowledge wisdom finds its throne.
All life-increasing arts to evil turn;
Where the mind makes the vital breath to burn,
(False) is the strength, (and o'er it we should
mourn.)

When things have become strong, they (then)
become old, which may
be said to be contrary to the Tao. Whatever is

contrary to the Tao
soon ends.

56

He who knows (the Tao) does not (care to) speak
(about it); he
who is (ever ready to) speak about it does not
know it.

He (who knows it) will keep his mouth shut and
close the portals
(of his nostrils). He will blunt his sharp points and
unravel the
complications of things; he will temper his
brightness, and bring
himself into agreement with the obscurity (of
others). This is called
'the Mysterious Agreement.'

(Such a one) cannot be treated familiarly or
distantly; he is
beyond all consideration of profit or injury; of
nobility or
meanness:--he is the noblest man under heaven.

57

A state may be ruled by (measures of) correction;
weapons of
war may be used with crafty dexterity; (but) the
kingdom is made one's
own (only) by freedom from action and purpose.

How do I know that it is so? By these facts:--In
the kingdom the
multiplication of prohibitive enactments increases
the poverty of the
people; the more implements to add to their profit
that the people
have, the greater disorder is there in the state and
clan; the more
acts of crafty dexterity that men possess, the more
do strange
contrivances appear; the more display there is of
legislation, the
more thieves and robbers there are.

Therefore a sage has said, 'I will do nothing (of
purpose), and the
people will be transformed of themselves; I will
be fond of keeping
still, and the people will of themselves become
correct. I will take
no trouble about it, and the people will of
themselves become rich; I
will manifest no ambition, and the people will of

themselves attain to
the primitive simplicity.'

58

The government that seems the most unwise,
Oft goodness to the people best supplies;
That which is meddling, touching everything,
Will work but ill, and disappointment bring.

Misery!--happiness is to be found by its side!
Happiness!--misery
lurks beneath it! Who knows what either will
come to in the end?

Shall we then dispense with correction? The
(method of) correction
shall by a turn become distortion, and the good in
it shall by a turn
become evil. The delusion of the people (on this
point) has indeed
subsisted for a long time.

Therefore the sage is (like) a square which cuts no
one (with its
angles); (like) a corner which injures no one (with
its sharpness).
He is straightforward, but allows himself no
license; he is bright,
but does not dazzle.

59

For regulating the human (in our constitution) and
rendering
the (proper) service to the heavenly, there is
nothing like
moderation.

It is only by this moderation that there is effected
an early
return (to man's normal state). That early return is
what I call the
repeated accumulation of the attributes (of the
Tao). With that
repeated accumulation of those attributes, there
comes the subjugation
(of every obstacle to such return). Of this
subjugation we know not
what shall be the limit; and when one knows not
what the limit shall
be, he may be the ruler of a state.

He who possesses the mother of the state may
continue long. His
case is like that (of the plant) of which we say that
its roots are
deep and its flower stalks firm:--this is the way to
secure that its
enduring life shall long be seen.

60

Governing a great state is like cooking small fish.

Let the kingdom be governed according to the
Tao, and the manes of
the departed will not manifest their spiritual
energy. It is not that
those manes have not that spiritual energy, but it
will not be
employed to hurt men. It is not that it could not
hurt men, but
neither does the ruling sage hurt them.

When these two do not injuriously affect each
other, their good
influences converge in the virtue (of the Tao).

61

What makes a great state is its being (like) a low-
lying, down-
flowing (stream);--it becomes the centre to which
tend (all the small
states) under heaven.

(To illustrate from) the case of all females:--the
female always
overcomes the male by her stillness. Stillness may
be considered (a
sort of) abasement.

Thus it is that a great state, by condescending to
small states,
gains them for itself; and that small states, by
abasing themselves to
a great state, win it over to them. In the one case
the abasement
leads to gaining adherents, in the other case to
procuring favor.

The great state only wishes to unite men together
and nourish them;
a small state only wishes to be received by, and to
serve, the other.
Each gets what it desires, but the great state must
learn to abase
itself.

62

Tao has of all things the most honored place.
No treasures give good men so rich a grace;
Bad men it guards, and doth their ill efface.

(Its) admirable words can purchase honor; (its)
admirable deeds
can raise their performer above others. Even men
who are not good are
not abandoned by it.

Therefore when the sovereign occupies his place
as the Son of
Heaven, and he has appointed his three ducal
ministers, though (a
prince) were to send in a round symbol-of-rank
large enough to fill
both the hands, and that as the precursor of the
team of horses (in
the court-yard), such an offering would not be
equal to (a lesson of)
this Tao, which one might present on his knees.

Why was it that the ancients prized this Tao so
much? Was it not
because it could be got by seeking for it, and the
guilty could escape
(from the stain of their guilt) by it? This is the
reason why all
under heaven consider it the most valuable thing.

63

(It is the way of the Tao) to act without (thinking
of) acting;
to conduct affairs without (feeling the) trouble of
them; to taste
without discerning any flavor; to consider what is
small as great,
and a few as many; and to recompense injury with
kindness.

(The master of it) anticipates things that are
difficult while they
are easy, and does things that would become great
while they are
small. All difficult things in the world are sure to
arise from a
previous state in which they were easy, and all
great things from one
in which they were small. Therefore the sage,
while he never does
what is great, is able on that account to
accomplish the greatest
things.

He who lightly promises is sure to keep but little
faith; he who is
continually thinking things easy is sure to find
them difficult.
Therefore the sage sees difficulty even in what
seems easy, and so
never has any difficulties.

64

That which is at rest is easily kept hold of; before
a thing
has given indications of its presence, it is easy to
take measures
against it; that which is brittle is easily broken;
that which is very
small is easily dispersed. Action should be taken
before a thing has
made its appearance; order should be secured
before disorder has
begun.

The tree which fills the arms grew from the tiniest
sprout; the
tower of nine storeys rose from a (small) heap of
earth; the journey
of a thousand li commenced with a single step.

He who acts (with an ulterior purpose) does harm;
he who takes hold
of a thing (in the same way) loses his hold. The
sage does not act
(so), and therefore does no harm; he does not lay
hold (so), and
therefore does not lose his bold. (But) people in
their conduct of
affairs are constantly ruining them when they are
on the eve of
success. If they were careful at the end, as (they
should be) at the

beginning, they would not so ruin them.

Therefore the sage desires what (other men) do
not desire, and does
not prize things difficult to get; he learns what
(other men) do not
learn, and turns back to what the multitude of men
have passed by.
Thus he helps the natural development of all
things, and does not dare
to act (with an ulterior purpose of his own).

65

The ancients who showed their skill in practicing
the Tao did
so, not to enlighten the people, but rather to make
them simple and
ignorant.

The difficulty in governing the people arises from
their having
much knowledge. He who (tries to) govern a state
by his wisdom is a
scourge to it; while he who does not (try to) do so
is a blessing.

He who knows these two things finds in them also
his model and
rule. Ability to know this model and rule
constitutes what we call
the mysterious excellence (of a governor). Deep
and far-reaching is
such mysterious excellence, showing indeed its
possessor as opposite
to others, but leading them to a great conformity
to him.

66

That whereby the rivers and seas are able to
receive the homage
and tribute of all the valley streams, is their skill
in being lower
than they;--it is thus that they are the kings of
them all. So it is
that the sage (ruler), wishing to be above men,
puts himself by his
words below them, and, wishing to be before
them, places his person
behind them.

In this way though he has his place above them,
men do not feel his
weight, nor though he has his place before them,
do they feel it an
injury to them.

Therefore all in the world delight to exalt him and
do not weary of
him. Because he does not strive, no one finds it
possible to strive
with him.

67

All the world says that, while my Tao is great, it
yet appears
to be inferior (to other systems of teaching). Now
it is just its
greatness that makes it seem to be inferior. If it
were like any
other (system), for long would its smallness have
been known!

But I have three precious things which I prize and
hold fast. The
first is gentleness; the second is economy; and the
third is shrinking
from taking precedence of others.

With that gentleness I can be bold; with that
economy I can be
liberal; shrinking from taking precedence of
others, I can become a
vessel of the highest honor. Now-a-days they give
up gentleness and
are all for being bold; economy, and are all for
being liberal; the
hindmost place, and seek only to be foremost;--(of
all which the end
is) death.

Gentleness is sure to be victorious even in battle,
and firmly to
maintain its ground. Heaven will save its

possessor, by his (very)
gentleness protecting him.

68

He who in (Tao's) wars has skill
Assumes no martial port;
He who fights with most good will
To rage makes no resort.
He who vanquishes yet still
Keeps from his foes apart;
He whose hests men most fulfil
Yet humbly plies his art.

Thus we say, 'He ne'er contends,
And therein is his might.'
Thus we say, 'Men's wills he bends,
That they with him unite.'
Thus we say, 'Like Heaven's his ends,
No sage of old more bright.'

69

A master of the art of war has said, 'I do not dare
to be the
host (to commence the war); I prefer to be the
guest (to act on the
defensive). I do not dare to advance an inch; I
prefer to retire a
foot.' This is called marshalling the ranks where
there are no ranks;
baring the arms (to fight) where there are no arms
to bare; grasping
the weapon where there is no weapon to grasp;
advancing against the
enemy where there is no enemy.

There is no calamity greater than lightly engaging
in war. To do
that is near losing (the gentleness) which is so
precious. Thus it is
that when opposing weapons are (actually)
crossed, he who deplores
(the situation) conquers.

70

My words are very easy to know, and very easy to
practice; but
there is no one in the world who is able to know
and able to practice
them.

There is an originating and all-comprehending
(principle) in my
words, and an authoritative law for the things
(which I enforce). It
is because they do not know these, that men do
not know me.

They who know me are few, and I am on that
account (the more) to be
prized. It is thus that the sage wears (a poor garb
of) hair cloth,
while he carries his (signet of) jade in his bosom.

71

To know and yet (think) we do not know is the highest
(attainment); not to know (and yet think) we do know is a disease.

It is simply by being pained at (the thought of) having this
disease that we are preserved from it. The sage has not the disease.
He knows the pain that would be inseparable from it, and therefore he
does not have it.

72

When the people do not fear what they ought to
fear, that which
is their great dread will come on them.

Let them not thoughtlessly indulge themselves in
their ordinary
life; let them not act as if weary of what that life
depends on.

It is by avoiding such indulgence that such
weariness does not
arise.

Therefore the sage knows (these things) of
himself, but does not
parade (his knowledge); loves, but does not
(appear to set a) value
on, himself. And thus he puts the latter alternative
away and makes
choice of the former.

73

He whose boldness appears in his daring (to do wrong, in
defiance of the laws) is put to death; he whose boldness appears in
his not daring (to do so) lives on. Of these two cases the one
appears to be advantageous, and the other to be injurious. But

When Heaven's anger smites a man,
Who the cause shall truly scan?

On this account the sage feels a difficulty (as to what to do in the
former case).

It is the way of Heaven not to strive, and yet it skillfully
overcomes; not to speak, and yet it is skillful in (obtaining a reply;
does not call, and yet men come to it of themselves. Its
demonstrations are quiet, and yet its plans are skillful and effective.
The meshes of the net of Heaven are large; far apart, but letting
nothing escape.

74

The people do not fear death; to what purpose is it
to (try to)
frighten them with death? If the people were
always in awe of death,
and I could always seize those who do wrong, and
put them to death,
who would dare to do wrong?

There is always One who presides over the
infliction death. He who
would inflict death in the room of him who so
presides over it may be
described as hewing wood instead of a great
carpenter. Seldom is it
that he who undertakes the hewing, instead of the
great carpenter,
does not cut his own hands!

75

The people suffer from famine because of the
multitude of taxes
consumed by their superiors. It is through this that
they suffer
famine.

The people are difficult to govern because of the
(excessive)
agency of their superiors (in governing them). It is
through this
that they are difficult to govern.

The people make light of dying because of the
greatness of their
labours in seeking for the means of living. It is
this which makes
them think light of dying. Thus it is that to leave
the subject of
living altogether out of view is better than to set a
high value on
it.

76

Man at his birth is supple and weak; at his death,
firm and
strong. (So it is with) all things. Trees and plants,
in their early
growth, are soft and brittle; at their death, dry and
withered.

Thus it is that firmness and strength are the
concomitants of
death; softness and weakness, the concomitants of
life.

Hence he who (relies on) the strength of his forces
does not
conquer; and a tree which is strong will fill the
out-stretched arms,
(and thereby invites the feller.)

Therefore the place of what is firm and strong is
below, and that
of what is soft and weak is above.

77

May not the Way (or Tao) of Heaven be
compared to the (method

of) bending a bow? The (part of the bow) which
was high is brought
low, and what was low is raised up. (So Heaven)
diminishes where
there is superabundance, and supplements where
there is deficiency.

It is the Way of Heaven to diminish
superabundance, and to
supplement deficiency. It is not so with the way of
man. He takes
away from those who have not enough to add to
his own superabundance.

Who can take his own superabundance and
therewith serve all under
heaven? Only he who is in possession of the Tao!

Therefore the (ruling) sage acts without claiming
the results as
his; he achieves his merit and does not rest
(arrogantly) in it:--he
does not wish to display his superiority.

78

There is nothing in the world more soft and weak
than water,
and yet for attacking things that are firm and
strong there is nothing
that can take precedence of it;--for there is
nothing (so effectual)
for which it can be changed.

Everyone in the world knows that the soft
overcomes the hard, and
the weak the strong, but no one is able to carry it
out in practice.

Therefore a sage has said,
'He who accepts his state's reproach,
Is hailed therefore its altars' lord;
To him who bears men's direful woes
They all the name of King accord.'

Words that are strictly true seem to be
paradoxical.

79

When a reconciliation is effected (between two
parties) after a
great animosity, there is sure to be a grudge
remaining (in the mind
of the one who was wrong). And how can this be
beneficial (to the
other)?

Therefore (to guard against this), the sage keeps
the left-hand
portion of the record of the engagement, and does
not insist on the
(speedy) fulfilment of it by the other party. (So),
he who has the
attributes (of the Tao) regards (only) the
conditions of the
engagement, while he who has not those attributes
regards only the
conditions favorable to himself.

In the Way of Heaven, there is no partiality of
love; it is always
on the side of the good man.

80

In a little state with a small population, I would so
order it,
that, though there were individuals with the
abilities of ten or a
hundred men, there should be no employment of
them; I would make the
people, while looking on death as a grievous
thing, yet not remove
elsewhere (to avoid it).

Though they had boats and carriages, they should
have no occasion
to ride in them; though they had buff coats and
sharp weapons, they
should have no occasion to don or use them.

I would make the people return to the use of
knotted cords (instead
of the written characters).

They should think their (coarse) food sweet; their
(plain) clothes
beautiful; their (poor) dwellings places of rest;
and their common
(simple) ways sources of enjoyment.

There should be a neighboring state within sight,
and the voices
of the fowls and dogs should be heard all the way
from it to us, but I

would make the people to old age, even to death,
not have any
intercourse with it.

81

Sincere words are not fine; fine words are not sincere. Those
who are skilled (in the Tao) do not dispute (about it); the
disputatious are not skilled in it. Those who know (the Tao) are not
extensively learned; the extensively learned do not know it.

The sage does not accumulate (for himself). The more that he
expends for others, the more does he possess of his own; the more that
he gives to others, the more does he have himself.

With all the sharpness of the Way of Heaven, it injures not; with
all the doing in the way of the sage he does not strive.